BETTY PARASKEVAS

GRACIE GRAVES AND THE KIDS FROM ROOM 402

ILLUSTRATED BY

Michael Paraskevas

Harcourt Brace & Company

SAN DIEGO NEW YORK LONDON

Library of Congress Cataloging-in-Publication Data
Paraskevas, Betty.
Gracie Graves and the kids from room 402/Betty Paraskevas; illustrated by Michael Paraskevas.—1st ed.
p. cm.
Summary: Brief humorous poems describe each of the fourteen boys and fourteen girls in Ms. Gracie Graves' class.
ISBN 0-15-200321-5
1. School children—Juvenile poetry. 2. Teachers—Juvenile poetry.
3. Schools—Juvenile poetry. 4. Children's poetry, American.
[1. Schools—Poetry. 2. American poetry. 3. Humorous poetry.]
I. Paraskevas, Michael, 1961–   ill. II. Title.
PS3566.A627G7   1995
811'.54—dc20   94-32661

First edition
A B C D E

Printed in Singapore

The jacket and title page display type was hand-lettered by the illustrator.
The text display type was set in Typewriter Bold.
The text type was set in Cheltenham.
This book was printed with soya-based inks on Leykam recycled paper, which contains more than 20 percent postconsumer waste and has a total recycled content of at least 50 percent.
Color separations were made by Bright Arts, Ltd., Singapore.
Printed and bound by Tien Wah Press, Singapore
Production supervision by Warren Wallerstein and David Hough
Designed by Michael Farmer

To Ronnie Conigliaro
and his wonderful boys;
Dean and Ryan,
and
to Aubrey Simpson...

All the world's a stage,
which explains why
there are so many flops.

—B. P. and M. P.

Gracie Graves

Gracie Graves had little silver curls,
Fourteen boys, and fourteen girls.
In thirty years she never forgot a name,
And her little silver curls stayed exactly the same.

Anna May Johnson

Anna May Johnson sat in the back.
She didn't need a reason to give a kid a whack.
She never did her homework. She never raised her hand.
Anna May Johnson played the tuba in the band.

Ray Tupper

Ray Tupper's dad was in the CIA.
The kids knew all about it; Ray told them every day.
But one day Ray ran out of luck
When his dad drove by in a vegetable truck.
The kids began to tease him, laughing at his lies.
Ray just bit his lip and said his dad was in disguise.

Lori Ann Tortelli

Lori Ann Tortelli always told the truth.
She told on Rachel Lily, Anna May, and Ruth.
When she was being truthful, her mouth would open wide.
She was telling Miss Graves the truth one day, and a fly flew right inside.

Vinnie Nasta

Eagle-eyed Gracie spied the answers to a quiz
Under Vinnie Nasta's desk. He said they weren't his.
But the evidence against him, she replied, was strong—
Since answers on his quiz and the paper both were wrong.

Nancy Francis

Nancy Francis was always in a tizzy.
Minding everybody's business kept her very busy.
She chewed on her pencils and twirled her curly hair.
Anna May Johnson put a thumbtack on her chair.

Freddie Fay

Freddie Fay made an awful smell
Mixing up a brew for show-and-tell.
He told everybody he could make perfume,
But it smelled like a polecat loose in the room.
It wilted the flowers
    and curled the map on the wall,
Wrapped the room in a shroud
    and moved out to the hall.
"HAIL TO OUR HERO, FREDDIE FAY!
    THEY CLOSED THE SCHOOL FOR THE REST OF THE DAY!"

Rachel Lily Bloomenthal

Rachel Lily Bloomenthal
Painted three-legged cats upon the wall.
A psychologist was summoned and promptly said,
"This child is disturbed. We must check out her head."
After hours of testing it was revealed that
Rachel Lily's family owned a three-legged cat.

Mary Ellen Devereaux

Mary Ellen Devereaux
Learned just one song for the talent show.
She won first prize playing "Lady of Spain,"
Then she left her accordion out in the rain.

Donald Boles

Every day Donald Boles
Brought egg salad for lunch on two hard rolls.
From the brown paper bag rose such an aroma,
Three comedians nearby fell into a coma.
The others all laughed; Gracie called them cruel
And kept the comatose kids after school.

Sally Spreen

Sally Spreen, the Beauty Queen.
Gracie called her a talking machine.
After school every day Sally served time,
Cleaning the blackboards to pay for her crime.

Molly and Polly McShane

Molly and Polly McShane were twins.
How cruel when Mother Nature sins:
Polly was pretty; Molly was not.
And Polly lost out on the brains Molly got.

Penny Grant

Penny Grant wore beautiful clothes.
She played the piano and danced on her toes.
She also spoke French, and every kid
Tried not to like her. But somehow they did.

Joey Tuna

Joey Tuna ate sixteen Twinkies
At the party on Halloween.
When the janitor arrived with a mop and pail,
It was the biggest mess he'd seen.
As Gracie led Joey down to the nurse,
He voiced his sad regret
For causing such an awful mess.
"I guess it was something I et."

Jenny Glover

Mr. Nickles raised his baton
For the fifteenth time, and the band played on.
The problem was always Jenny Glover—
When the music stopped, she had a note left over.

Ruthie Drew

Little Ruthie Drew dropped her valentines
Into a box on the shelf.
She had quite a few, but nobody knew
She sent them all to herself.

Robert Spence

Robert Spence was a whiz at math.
Gracie sent him home with a note to take a bath.
His clothes didn't fit. He was quiet and shy.
But the kids never teased him, and Gracie knew why.
Robert Spence was a whiz, and there never was a doubt:
When kids were stuck on math,
    Robert Spence would help them out.

Tillie Ferillo

Tillie Ferillo took a pussy willow
   and stuffed it up her nose.
She sniffled and wheezed,
   and every time she sneezed,
   Gracie lost the petals off a rose.
But Tillie wouldn't tell
   till her nose began to swell.
They rushed her to the doctor straight from school.
The doctor poked about. It took an hour to get it out.
She said he used a Roto-Rooter tool.

Anna Shannon

Anna Shannon left her bubble gum
On one of the chairs in the gymnasium.
When the principal rose to address the class,
Anna Shannon's bubble gum stuck to his... *trousers*.

Piggy McCall

"Dodge ball, dodge ball!"
Let's sing a song of Piggy McCall.
He'd try to run but was always the one
Who got hit with the ball while we had the fun
Singing, *"Dodge ball, dodge ball!"*

Andy Fox

Andy Fox had a coonskin hat.
Louie Bona killed it with a baseball bat.
Louie swore it chased him—
    It jumped right off the shelf.
Gracie Graves said, "Louie Bona, try to redeem yourself."
So Louie Bona buried the hat under a willow tree.
He marked the grave with a sign that read:
It Was Either the Hat or Me.
The kids all thought it was funny, except for Andy Fox,
But he got even with Louie—he gave him the chicken pox.

Billy Boyle

Billy gave a book report
   on a book he hadn't read.
He couldn't comment on the story,
   So he reviewed the cover instead.
He discussed the number of pages
   and the author's photograph.
Gracie told him to get to the point,
   and the kids began to laugh.
With one eye on the clock,
   he continued to repeat
How much he really liked the book,
   then bowed and took his seat.

Margie Petrowsky

Margie Petrowsky was a chubby-plus.
Two boys liked to tease her every day on the bus.
Anna May Johnson, who sat in the back
And didn't need a reason to give a kid a whack,
Felt the milk of human kindness stir in her one day
As she watched Margie struggle to wipe her tears away.
It only took one blow to send both boys to defeat,
Then Anna May Johnson silently took her seat.

Timmy O'Rourke

Timmy O'Rourke told the class that a stork
    had brought him a new baby brother.
All the kids snickered, and Gracie suggested
    he go home and check with his mother.
When Timmy got back—alas and alack!—
    he admitted he had been mistaken,
And held up a head of cabbage from
    the patch where his brother'd been taken.

Jesse McCoy

Listen to the music of Jesse McCoy,
Wearing long pants made of brown corduroy.
On his way to the blackboard they go *zit-zit-zit*.
When the bell rings, his tempo picks up quite a bit.

Charlie Cole

When Gracie Graves called the roll
And she didn't get an answer from Charlie Cole,
She'd say, "Anna May Johnson, go check the other classes.
Lordy, that child has forgotten his glasses."

Randy Brown

Every day when the clock struck two,
Randy raised his hand and all the others knew
He had to use the boys' room. As the kids watched him scurry,
Everybody shouted out, "Hurry, Randy, hurry!"

Arthur Kenneth Vanderwall

Arthur Kenneth Vanderwall—
The new kid in class with a southern drawl.
He had blond, wavy hair and carried a comb.
Every day Arthur walked another girl home.

School's Out

On the last day of school the kids in Gracie's class
Gathered together to see if they'd pass.

Gracie took a picture of the kids in 402....
Which one is me and which one is you?